Commute Encounters

From one place to another

Lindsay Jacobsen

Copyright © Lindsay Jacobsen, 2021

All right reserved. No part of this book may be reproduced or used in any manner without written permission of the copyright owner.

Book Design
Jaclyn Zatorski

Chapter Photos
via Unsplash - Mohammad Rezaie, Lorimcm, Quin Stevenson, Luka Vovk, Shifaz Mohmmed, Jon Tyson, Raul Gonzalez, Escobar, Parker Johnson, Varun Gaba, Suhyeon Choi, Daniel Chekalov, Aaron Burden, Austin Kehmeier, Filip Zrnzević

Special Thanks
Jonathan Kamper & Sylvia Zuiderveen

Commute Encounters

Foreword

Every now and then you know you've been ridiculously blessed to be a part of something that is simply extraordinary. Something so impactful and tender you find yourself a bit giddy that you've witnessed the magnificent process come to fruition.

That's where I find myself right now as I write this foreword. The amazing book you hold in your hands is a tremendous look into the life of a gal so radically connected to Jesus she can't hold back her joy. This book is overflowing with reasons to praise God and see His glory so evident in both the mountaintops and the mundane of our day to day lives.

It is so easy to discount the many opportunities we have in our daily routine to recall and remember God's handiwork through the people, events, and objects all around us. This book will challenge and encourage you to ponder and proclaim the many ways God reveals His goodness to you. Lindsay shares how her windshield time on her daily commute to work is packed with valuable lessons and reminders to declare God's glory.

Friend, as you read this you will laugh, cry, and find encouragement in the steadfast love and faithfulness of a God who cares personally and provisionally for you. You will be drawn in to praise and adoration for

God's miraculous and tender grace showcased in the pages of this book. You will be captivated by the book more and more each day as you find yourself relating to the struggles, joys, exhaustions, and experiences so vulnerably shared. Lindsay has found the joy of living transparently to make much of the work God has done in her life. Each story will fuel your hope in God's creative care for His own with a fresh confidence in how He alone satisfies, heals, redeems, and restores us.

Grab a cup of coffee, find a comfy chair, and join me in daily adventures beckoning us to praise God for His unending loving kindness!

Joyful to share this journey with you,

Sylvia Zuiderveen

Commute Encounters

Contents

- Welcome P.8
- From a Flag.. P.11
- From a Grocery List.. P.18
- From Dogs... P.27
- From a Storm... P.37
- From a Yard.. P.48
- From a Mother.. P.56
- From a Red Light.. P.65
- From CDs... P.73
- From a Song... P.82
- From a Scar.. P.90
- From Poop P.100
- From a Dream... P.109
- From a Deer... P.119
- From a Stranger... P.127
- Dear Reader... P.138

Welcome to Commute Encounters!

I am so thrilled that you are here! I have spent countless hours composing this book you now possess, and I am so excited to share about my encounters with you. Before we get to me, I want to talk about you! Who are you, reader? Why have you picked up my book? Did you pick it up because you know me personally, and you're showing support? Are we friends? Acquaintances? Strangers? Whatever the case may be, I am so glad that you are here.

If you've ever held a job of any sort, chances are good you have experienced a commute at some point in your life. By "commute", I mean you have traveled from your home to a workplace of some sort. Having held multiple jobs in the past 15+ years, I have grown to see just about every sort of encounter you could possibly have on your daily commute. Many of those experiences have been pleasant, but I've also had my fair share of hiccups. Regardless of the experience, I began to notice the gentle lessons the Lord was trying to teach me along the way.

Through some advice from friends and guidance from the Lord, I have decided to compile some of my commute experiences, which you now possess in the pages you hold in your hands. I pray that you, dear reader, find relatability and encouragement in these pages. I pray that you feel the presence of the Lord within these pages. Most of all, I pray that you develop a deepening desire to use every experience from your own commute time for the glory of God.

I'd like to extend a huge thank you to those who have supported me on this newfound journey of writing: my incredible husband, Jeremiah, my parents, my family, my friends, and my church community at Coram Deo. Thank you for your support and encouragement.

To my son, Samuel, I pray that through this journey of compiling these moments, I will have a renewed spirit to be a guide and light to you. All throughout this life, I promise to always point you back to the Lord. I love you, buddy.

Finally, and most importantly, this book would not be possible without the presence of Jesus Christ in my life. I pray that the following pages will be a clear reflection of who He is, and I pray that all who read this, will have a growing desire to pursue Him.

Lindsay Jacobsen

- HOW TO GET THE MOST OUT OF THIS BOOK -

Each chapter will begin with a few select Scripture references. While it can be easy to pass them over and get to the content, my desire is for you to take the time to look up the Scripture mentioned before reading the chapter. In fact, I ask that you don't even turn the page until you have looked up and read the provided Scripture. It will prepare your heart for the following experience, and leave you with the mindset to receive the application as best as possible.

Secondly, you will find a prayer section at the end of each chapter. I urge you to pray through the words I have left for you there. I also urge you to truly dwell on what the Lord has revealed to you during the chapter, and to write out your own prayer. This is so important, and it is a wonderful place for you to be honest with the Lord. Please take advantage of it.

OH WAIT! ONE LAST THING!

As you read through my commute encounters, you are sure to notice some punctuation and grammar errors. One of my favorite parts about this collection of experiences is the rawness and vulnerability of them. I want you to feel like I'm sitting right beside you, speaking these chapters to you as if we're close friends. Formality is nice and all, but that is not the goal of this book. The goal is for you to receive the words I have written in a similarly raw fashion as the moment in which they happened. I ask for your grace ahead of time, and I trust you will walk away from this book as though you've known me your whole life – grammar errors and all.

Commute Encounters

From a Flag

SCRIPTURE

*John 16:33, Romans 12:2, Romans 12:21,
Matthew 5:13-16*

There were so many questions and controversies during the year 2020. Not only was America in the middle of the COVID-19 pandemic, but the entire world felt rattled. With so much uncertainty, and fear within the year, I'd find it hard to believe that anyone would ever forget what went down in 2020.

Strangers were fighting each other over toilet paper in the stores. People were lining up at gas stations, willingly waiting for well over an hour for their turn at a pump. Half the country argued the necessity for everyone to be on lock-down. The other half grumbled at the idea of staying idle. Many complied with the idea of facemasks, while others saw it as unnecessary.

Politics and celebrities took cheap shots at each other. Neighbors began turning their backs on one another. Riots and protests broke out all over the country, with "Justice!" being the battle cry. Students all over the country were missing out on their school proms and sporting events. New mothers in the hospital were left alone, as their families were blocked from seeing their precious new additions.

Truly, all of this was a disheartening nightmare for the soul to see.

Social media was a whole battleground of its own. My heart ached at seeing what some of my fellow Jesus followers were posting. I had never seen so many of my friends place their trust in the government, their own pride, or science. The number of arguments that continually broke out was pitiful, and full of sin. My own sly tongue admittingly participating on occasion.

Through conversations with my family and friends, all I could do was be hopeful and trust that they would try to stay positive in their circumstances. That's all anyone could do during that time – stay hopeful.

Growing up, I was fortunate enough to say the Pledge of Allegiance in my Elementary School classrooms each morning, with my hand over my heart. From those early days of my life, I've found that I have an instilled sense of pride and empowerment whenever I see the American flag. My love for our country runs deep, and I am reminded of that every time I see those stars and stripes. My husband has been deployed in the military, and still remains in the National Guard. I am incredibly proud of him, and that makes the pride for my country run even deeper.

One morning on my drive to work, I drove by a home that had a large flagpole displayed. However, instead of an American flag, there was a homemade, custom flag flying high. It appeared to be a simple sheet of cloth, with a spray-painted message on it. The flag read, "We Are F**ked!".

I briefly choked on my coffee and had to do a double take, as my eyes were in pure disbelief. I could not wrap my mind around how someone could replace the American flag with something like that. It was an incredibly distasteful sight, and it shattered my hopeful heart and American pride. I was so angry with what I had seen, I could barely drive straight. A foul taste grew in my mouth, and a particular kind of rage grew in my heart. The temptation to turn around and go confront the homeowner was overwhelming.

That's when I took a deep breath and turned my eyes skyward. All I could do in that moment was take a deep breath and pray. Fortunately, it did not take long before I felt the Holy Spirit encompass me and bring a rejuvenating sense of peace.

As I continued driving to work, I reminded myself that my hope was in the Lord, not in the American flag. God has control of this country, not the government or the American people, even though it doesn't always appear that way.

Why should I be surprised when I see the world acting worldly? We live in a broken, sinful world and it has been that way since the days of Adam and Eve. Sure, I could go back and tear down that flag or confront the homeowner, but what good would that do? It would settle an itch I have, but it wouldn't solve anything past that. My prideful ambition is not enough to win the spiritual warfare of this country.

Jesus has already won the war for us by dying sacrificially on the cross in our place. Our country needs more prayer. Our country needs more Jesus. Lord, forgive me for thinking I need to fight the battle for you.

INVITE HIM IN

It's hard to be still when you see any form of injustice. As easy as it would be to act now and think later, we absolutely *must* remember that the war is in God's hands and not ours. This does not mean we can just sit back and watch as the world and its people slowly deteriorate. We must use discernment to analyze and wisely pick and choose which specific battles the Lord has called us to. I urge you, reader, stand firm in your faith and the truth of God's Word. Like an unmovable tree with deep roots, we too can be anchored in the Lord.

Today, I challenge you to focus your mind on the endgame. Look to the promises that Scripture gives us for the future, and for our reserved place in heaven. As the days on earth approach the end, we will see more and more darkness. Be on guard and protect your spirit. Be on guard and remain hopeful and watchful. Reflect on what you can do today – right now – to not only repel the darkness, but to also combat it. How can you be a beacon of light and serve as a reflection of Christ?

1._____

_____

2._____

_____

PRAYER

Lord God, thank You for this country. Thank You for giving us this land of freedom, even when it seems like a lost nation. I pray that You reveal Yourself to those who need to see You the most right now, myself included. Win this world back, Lord. We trust in You alone, and we trust in Your great plan. Thank You for sending Your son to die in our place, so that we can have an unshakeable freedom found in You and only You. We trust in You always, Lord. We love You and praise You. Amen.

PRAYER
(write your own)

_____
_____
_____
_____
_____
_____
_____
_____
_____
_____
_____

Commute Encounters

From a Grocery List

SCRIPTURE

James 1:2-3, Isaiah 40:31, Psalm 66:10-12, Matthew 6:25-27

Having recently entered into motherhood, I often feel overwhelmed. My to-do list seems to grow longer and longer by the day, with no end in sight. I've learned the hard way that while caring for a little one, there are other things in your life that will be placed on the backburner or simply overseen altogether.

During one of my morning commutes, all I could think about was groceries. I usually have our groceries delivered to our house once a week, but I was about two weeks behind and I felt like a failure. I was trying not to cry on my drive to work that day, and I was actively working to convince myself that my husband and four-month-old son would indeed be okay and not starve to death.

I shook the fear and anxiety off as I drove into the church parking lot and sat there, pulling myself back to reality. The overthinking and exaggeration I had just experienced was a result of pure hormone imbalance. I had just recently returned to work from maternity leave, and I tell you what - postpartum hormones are *real*. They don't just make you experience a fluctuation of emotions, but they can have a real mental impact on a new mother.

My husband and I discovered we were expecting in February of 2020, right before the COVID-19 outbreak happened. When the pandemic began to spread that next month, we heard all sorts of warnings, dangers, and restrictions for pregnant women. I couldn't share my pregnancy announcement in person with friends and some family, and I had to go to many doctor appointments alone. The feeling of isolation was beginning to settle in for me.

Then, it was time for my husband to travel to Texas and Alabama for three months due to military training. In his absence, our water heater and air conditioner both went out. We also had our roof replaced, and then the Iowa derecho happened (good timing!). Thanks to the derecho and the damage it brought, I ended up without power in my home for nine days. To say the least, it was a struggle - especially with my husband being gone, and the rest of my family and friends having visiting restrictions. Oh, and did I mention I was *very* pregnant?

Finally, in October of 2020, my son was born. My husband had returned home the month prior, and he and I were ready to enter into parenthood. It was one of the best days of my life, but more on that in a later chapter. Hang tight!

After my son's arrival, I was on maternity leave until early February. Through those winter months, it felt like my postpartum hormones were out to sabotage me. My anxiety got the best of me during those first couple months of motherhood, and I eventually began dealing with panic attacks. These panic attacks became a regular occurrence, leading me down a darker and darker road each time I would have one. My son was barely over a month old at the time, and I became so tormented over whether I could care for him or not. I doubted myself, and began to doubt my existence in the world.

"Maybe this place would be better off without me."

As much as it pains me to type the words, I doubted my son's existence in the world too.

Maybe he was a mistake. Do I really want him?

When these attacks happened, the thoughts that would flood my mind were so incredibly evil. They reverberated hopelessness, pure darkness, and sin. It was a very scary place to be. It breaks my heart to even have to write these things.

I would cry out to God with all that I was, and yet, I would receive silence. I remember falling on my hands and knees weeping, begging the Lord to deliver me from this darkness. Nothing happened. I would sit on the floor in my shower and let the scalding hot water wash over me, hiding my tears of utter defeat.

My poor husband felt helpless, and my parents were crushed at some of the things I would say during these attacks. I remember in one instance, I sat on my kitchen floor just sobbing uncontrollably, with my husband and parents close by, watching. Nothing they said or did could provide any tangible help in the moment, but I do vividly recall them telling me how much they loved me, and how the person I became during these attacks wasn't the "real me".

As the days passed by with no improvement for me, my husband and parents decided it'd be best if I wasn't left alone anymore, especially overnight. My husband is a firefighter and works 24-hour shifts, so the plan would be for me and my son to stay at my parent's house on the nights when he was working. It felt so incredibly embarrassing to need that kind of intentional help, but I was in a very dark place. It felt like God had exited from my life, and honestly, I didn't trust myself.

Over time, I got the physical help that I needed. I have been blessed with a wise and patient family doctor who guided me through the right balance of medication, exercise, and establishing a solid support system within my family and church. It took a few months to stabilize, but I am so incredibly thankful to report I am in a much better place today.

Do I still struggle on some days? *Yes.*

Do I still fear that another panic attack will happen and I'll return to that dark place? *Of course.*

Do I know who holds my life in His hands? *You bet.*

All glory be to God. Even in my deepest, darkest days, I know He never truly left me. He will never leave me. It's almost comical to me that it took my thinking through a grocery list to recall these events, and that the Lord provides, sustains, and delivers.

Have you ever felt like that, reader? The feeling of despair, like God has completely abandoned you? It is a feeling and emotion like no other; quite honestly, it is one that hurts and shakes you to your core. Of course, the most important part of that feeling of abandonment is this: it is an absolute and complete <u>lie</u> that we <u>must</u> take captive. The Lord does not abandon. While it is true that we may endure trials and trying times to be sharpened and refined, we are never forgotten.

As I continued to sit in the church parking lot reflecting on all of these thoughts, the idea of my grocery list not being complete suddenly seemed so inconsequential. I mean, here I was on the brink of tears over a simple incomplete grocery list.

When Jesus proved His overwhelming love for me on the cross, did he not also prove that he would always sustain and take care of me? When I was delivered from those dark days of postpartum, was that not proof enough of the extent of His love for me? Why would I not trust Him to fill my family's table? Oh Lord, I'm sorry. How could I have forgotten so easily?

INVITE HIM IN

It's hard when we come face to face with difficult trials, and it can be easy to feel like we are on our own. Even with the support of friends, family and loved ones, the burden we bear still feels inescapable at times. What trial has been present in your life lately? Perhaps your trial is a physical one that involves a heartbreaking loss or diagnosis. Maybe it's an emotional trial that breaks your heart in a different kind of way. Take the time to think of a trial right now in your life. Do you have it? Okay, good. Now here's what you do. This is crucial. **CLING** to the fact that you are not meant to bear this trial burden alone. Jesus made that promise to you when He died on the cross in your place. He is the ultimate Sustainer, Redeemer, and Helper.

Today, I challenge you turn your trial over to the Lord. Don't just pray about it, but actually *surrender* it. Release it from your hands and watch what God does next. I pray, sweet friend, that you will be tremendously blessed through your faith in doing that. Take some time right now to pray over your trial. Then, take a sheet of paper and write your trial on it. Write as much about it as you want. When you're done, read it over in its entirety, then shred it up and trash it. Pray again over it, and trust that the Lord will take it from there.

PRAYER

Father God, I admit, I have my struggles to wrestle with. I know I shouldn't rely on my own strength through my trials, but my sinful self tends to default to that. I will surrender these habits and trials to You now, and I fully trust in You and Your plan for my life. Please help me to remember that You are in control, and that I can rest in that blessed promise. Thank You for sending Your son, Jesus, to be sacrificed in my place. That act alone ensures that I don't have to face my trials alone. I praise Your name for Your endless love, Father. Amen.

PRAYER
(write your own)

_____

_____

_____

_____

_____

_____

_____

_____

_____

Commute Encounters

From Dogs

SCRIPTURE

Romans 14:13, Galatians 6:1-5, 1 Thessalonians 5:11, Proverbs 27:17

When you travel 45 minutes to and from work every day through rural Iowa, you're bound to encounter animals. Each morning I have the joy of driving past farmers on their tractors, as they haul breakfast out to their cattle in the morning. I chuckle as I see goats being chased by their kids (no pun intended), as a playful "good morning" to each other. I get to see horses stretch out their legs in the morning air, breathing in the new day.

Of all those things, my favorite part would have to be seeing the new babies in these animal families grow as the seasons change.

On occasion, I also get to see wildlife on my commute. I've had my fair share of raccoon, opossum, deer and coyote encounters; mostly in the form of unexpected braking or swerving. Due to the unpredictability of the wildlife, I have learned to constantly scan my eyes across the roadway.

I didn't *always* do this sort of scanning of my surroundings. I had to learn the hard way a time or two, which you will read about a little bit later. One of my more memorable animal encounters included a pair of dogs. As I would drive down a particular rural road, a pair of dogs would emerge from behind a house and run alongside the road in pursuit of my car. The first time it happened, it terrified me. I had hit the brakes and waited for impact, but nothing happened. I looked out of my window and saw two little heads peering back at me, waiting for me to accelerate again. So, I did. Then I did the next day, and the next. It was a playful chase, and I found myself looking forward to "racing" them every morning. This went on for weeks, and as each day passed, they'd move slightly closer and closer to the pavement. They seemed to be getting braver – more confident.

The days went on and every single morning those dogs would appear. It became the new norm for me during my drive, and pretty soon I found myself on auto-pilot. I no longer thought twice about the potential danger of our game.

One day as I approached that house, I gripped my steering wheel and prepared for the day's race. I arrived at the house and yet, neither dog appeared. I shrugged it off, assumed they were inside, and went on my merry way. The next day came, and once again, neither dog appeared; nor the next day, or the next.

My mind naturally started to wander, and I gulped as my thoughts went to the worst outcome. After all, they were very brave, bold dogs. Maybe I wasn't the only vehicle that they challenged to a race. Perhaps another driver wasn't paying attention and didn't notice the dogs as they made their way onto the pavement.

Those next couple of weeks as I drove to work, I still watched and waited expectantly for them. Even now, years later, I still find myself glancing at that house as I pass by. I never saw those dogs again.

I wonder if by now you have had similar thoughts to mine:

"Did those dogs end up getting hit?"

"Why didn't the owners keep a better eye on them?"

"Why did you encourage such dangerous behavior?"

As much as I enjoyed our impromptu game, it ultimately (on pure assumption) had a permanent impact on the lives of those dogs and their owner. Looking back, as much as I want to blame the owners for their lack of discipline towards their dogs, I also must assume a bit of responsibility myself. I still struggle to accept the idea that they are (probably) no longer alive.

I admit, it took me days to process this particular encounter and analyze what the Lord could possibly be revealing to me in this moment, if anything. I finally turned to Scripture and sought out any sort of verse that would enlighten me.

The biggest theme that appeared to be reoccurring in my mind was "accountability". The owner of those dogs had a responsibility to ensure and encourage their safety and discipline. I had the obligation as a driver to make sure I was driving safely and responsibly for myself and those around me. This last one may be a bit of a stretch, but I would even say those dogs had a sense of responsibility to each other. If even one of them had resisted the impulse to chase cars, the other probably would have followed suit.

All three instances are a reflection of accountability in one way or another, which no party involved upheld. If even one of those instances had occurred, I believe those dogs would still be around.

Bringing my wandering mind back to my own life, I reflected on having been in all three of those positions myself at some point or another. First, I have had influence over others and led them negatively. Secondly, I've put myself in dangerous situations by not resisting temptation. Thirdly, I have been a third party on the sidelines who passively encouraged the unhealthy behavior of another by not intervening or speaking up.

I write these words and can recall the specific names of people in my life who have been impacted by me in one of those three situations. Heartache and regret have been the result in most cases, and some of that I still carry with me to this day.

Accountability is such an easy concept to grasp, but it can be an incredibly heavy one to implement. Sometimes fear prevents accountability. Fear of confronting a loved one, or perhaps a fear of judgement or retaliation. Sometimes we put up a roadblock in order to sustain our own selfish desire. Either way, we can bank on our lack of accountability playing a role one way or another; positive or negative.

One concept that keeps accountability in a powerful perspective for me is the idea of doing it out of love. When we lovingly approach each other with gentle accountability or correction, we can have the peacefulness that it will be received well. If we approach it with judgement, harshness or pride in our hearts, then we can bank on our so called "accountability" to be met with resistance. Motives here are everything, and so incredibly important.

Looking at our lives as striving to be an example of Jesus, we can cling to the fact that we are called to act out of love. It was love that made God send His son to us. It was love that held Jesus to the cross in our place. It was love that conquered death and rose again three days later.

With that kind of overwhelming love as our example, imagine what our world would look like if we let love be the motivation for our words and actions. Surely then, we would not hesitate to pursue loving accountability for ourselves and for one another.

INVITE HIM IN

What an incredible world we would live in if we chose to be bold enough to hold others accountable. Whether that be due to a form of injustice or personal accountability, we ought to have the overwhelming desire to support and restore one another. We ought to love one another unconditionally, and do whatever we can in our own realm of possibility to help a brother or sister. Isn't that exactly what Jesus did for us?

Today, I challenge you to examine your own life, specifically in light of Romans 14:13. Is there anything you are doing or saying that could have a negative influence on a fellow follower of Christ? Are you causing anyone else to stumble? At the end of the day, we are not responsible for the choices of another. However, we all have the responsibility to take an active role in not being a tool to cultivate sin. On the following page is a list of examples of potential stumbling blocks for yourself or others. Not all are sinful, but they can become a foothold for danger. Take some time to read through the list and prayerfully (and honestly) consider if you partake in any of these things that could cause another to stumble. Choose today as a starting point to faithfully follow Christ and put to death any areas that are a danger to you or others.

Which of these have or are you struggling with? Circle them below and decide now that you are going to put Jesus first. Take a picture of this page if you need to. Tear it out and stick it in your bible, if necessary. Don't forget this goal, and trust that God will help you overcome it.

Abuse	Fear	Lying
Alcohol	Gluttony	Power Hungry
Anger	Gossip	Pride
Anxiety	Greed	Revenge
Apathy	Guilt	Selfishness
Bitterness	Hypocrisy	Sexuality
Blasphemy	Idolatry	Slander
Cheating	Impatience	Smoking
Cursing	Jealousy	Stubbornness
Disrespect	Judging	Wealth
Drugs	Laziness	Worry
Envy	Lust	Wrath

Other: _____

_____

What are you going to do about it? _____

_____

_____

_____

PRAYER

Father, I don't want to be the reason another believer stumbles. I know Your grace is more than enough to cover us, but I know I also play a role in progressing your Kingdom. Instill in me a renewed passion to build up my fellow brothers and sisters in Christ. Give me the strength and courage to address those around me if I should see them in sin. I lift up the things I circled on the previous page and surrender them to You. I know You are able. Give me wisdom to maneuver through these days, Lord. All for Your glory. Amen.

PRAYER
(write your own)

_____
_____
_____
_____
_____
_____
_____
_____

Commute Encounters

From a Storm

SCRIPTURE
Isaiah 41:10, Psalm 27:1-3, Psalm 34:4

I have never considered myself to be a fearful person. Sure, there were things that would give me a spook when I was a kid such as scary movies and haunted houses, but nothing specific would ever come to mind when I was asked what I was afraid of. Fast forward to the summer of 2014 when I would be faced with a near death experience that instilled a new fear in me: thunderstorms.

That summer I was part of a church mission trip team that traveled to Booneville, Arkansas. Our team was made up of 12 individuals, comprised primarily of adults and high school students. We stayed in Arkansas for a little less than a week, doing various work projects and we also helped run a children's program. It was an incredible experience, but by the end of the week, I was ready to be home.

As we departed for home, our group of three vehicles drove caravan-style on the highway. My vehicle was the middle car and was packed with snacks, good music, and one of my closest friends in the passenger seat. We had our head pastor's son, and another good friend in the backseat. It was the perfect recipe for a good time, and we were here for it.

Then, the thunderstorm came.

My co-pilot checked his phone weather radar and we saw a giant red blob directly in our path. It was raining so hard and the drops were so thick, that our visibility was reduced to only about 25 feet. Vehicles were pulling off to the side of the road, and the rain drowned out all other sounds, demanding our full attention. I've driven in bad weather before and took all the necessary precautions to keep my passengers and myself safe.

We got a small break from the downpour when we arrived at the Bobby Hopper Tunnel. Our surroundings were darkened even more as we entered the tunnel. The dim yellow ceiling lights highlighted our path, and the soft echo of the rain outside bounced off the tunnel walls, creating an eerie atmosphere. Our car was silent as we made our way through, seeing the end of the tunnel come closer and closer.

When we finally emerged, it felt like driving into a waterfall. The sudden thump of water on the windshield was startling, and the darkness of the sky surrounded us once again. Within seconds, I felt myself lose control of the car. My hands were straight on the steering wheel, but I could feel the car slowly gliding to the right. I could barely see anything, but I spared a sliver of a second to cast a side-eye at my friend next to me.

"Lindsay..." he said.

"...I know." I responded.

In that blink of a moment, we were suddenly no longer gliding. Oh no, no. Now we were full on hydroplaning towards the cliff side on the right of the highway. Oh yeah, did I mention there were still several cars that had pulled over and parked along that side? I gripped the steering wheel and braced for impact. Yet, the impact did not come. Somehow the car had regained traction and swerved to the left at the last second to avoid a massive accident.

I blinked for a brief second again, and now realized the vehicle was still moving, but now we were headed right for the concrete barrier separating us and oncoming traffic. All I could imagine in that moment was that we were about to hit that barrier, and flip the car over into the oncoming traffic on the other side.

I was prepared for my death. I knew it was coming, and I was ready to accept that I had made a deadly mistake.

This all happened in a matter of seconds, and yet it felt like time stood still. I was reflecting on my lapse of judgement in this instance, and I prepared to meet Jesus. I thought of the words I would say to Him, and the apology I would need to extend covering the souls of those three other individuals in the car with me. I was prepared and not prepared all at the same time to meet our King.

I closed my eyes, perhaps muttered a slur under my breath, and braced for impact.

Once again, it didn't come. I drew in a sharp breath and opened my tear-filled eyes. I was driving straight again! The car was stable, and I once again had full control. My jaw dropped open, and I was in a state of shock and pure disbelief. I glanced at my companions; their postures were stiff, and their expressions identical to mine.

Even all these years later, I can still recall the events of that day like it was yesterday. The terror I experienced has rocked and followed me to the present. Every time

I hear rain or thunder, I can't help but shudder. My panicked mind immediately thinks the worst when I know a storm is approaching my area. My mind goes to tornadoes, apocalyptic-like storms, and even death.

It's a grueling inner-body experience when I know a storm is coming. It's even worse when I find myself in the midst of a storm, with no way out.

During one of my nightly commutes, I had no choice but to drive home through a thunderstorm. It was a Wednesday night, which meant I'd be at the church until probably 9pm or so. I had been keeping an eye on the weather radar all day, and had tried to map out a plan for the approaching storm and what I should do. The timing of the storm fluctuated throughout the day, but, naturally, it decided to arrive right when it was time for me to drive home.

My husband was in his truck ahead of me with my younger cousin with him. They were also leaving the church, so I decided I would just follow behind them on the drive home. Sounds a bit familiar, right?

My husband, being the wonderful, law-abiding human that he is, drove the speed limit. In fact, he drove a little *under* the speed limit due to the poor weather. What a guy, but I tell you what. It was driving me absolutely insane. My fear-driven fight or flight instinct was churning deep within my stomach, and all I wanted to do was speed through this storm as fast as humanly possible. The faster we drive, the faster we get home. The faster we get home, the less of the storm we have to experience. It makes total, logical, non-irrational sense. Right?

As I continued puttering along behind my husband's truck, my mind felt like one giant fog cloud. In this moment, for whatever reason, I was now going over the speed limit and passing my husband. The rain was so thick, I couldn't even see into his window as I passed, although I'm sure he was quite baffled at my actions.

Now that I didn't have his truck to follow as a guide, I was relying solely on my GPS to tell me where the road was going. I prayed that no animal or other vehicle would be in my path, as surely, I would have no time to brake for it. It was a risk I was willing to take if it meant I could get home even a few seconds earlier.

From having traveled these back country roads hundreds of times over the years, I knew exactly where houses would be as I passed. I even flirted with the idea at stopping at one of them to seek shelter. The fear of approaching a stranger's home made more sense to me in that moment than to continue driving. This, of course, was the panic in me speaking.

Eventually I did make it home safely, as did my husband and cousin. We serve a good God who even in my stupid, panicked driven decision-making, allowed me to arrive home safely. I definitely do not condone the actions I took in either experience, and it's by the pure grace of God that I made it through both unscathed. While I admit that I am still quite fearful of storms, I personally now the Creator of the storms.

After more time has passed from that event, I have had it impressed upon me even more that the Lord can always be sought out to deliver us from our fears. Our fears don't have to control us, nor should we allow for them to. The Lord is bigger than our fears, and desires for us to surrender them to him. If we chose to lean into that more, just imagine how much more our faith and trust would flourish and glorify him.

INVITE HIM IN

If we let our guard down, it can be incredibly easy to let our emotions have too big of an impact on our lives. Sometimes they can control us so much, that our every word and action is defined by it. While many emotions are healthy and beneficial for us to feel and experience, fear is one that is quite up for debate in the world of Christianity. Scripture is littered with references of being told to "fear not" or "do not be afraid". In fact, take a minute to look up how many times the Bible mentions "fear" – you'll probably be quite surprised! It's not a topic the Lord withdraws from, but rather leans into and addresses boldly. If the Lord feels so strongly about it, perhaps it is something we need to lean into more as well.

Today, I challenge you to identify a fear in your life that you need to surrender to God. There are plenty of tangible things that can make us fearful (storms, clowns, snakes, the dark, etc.). Once you have a fear selected, I want you to dive deeper into it. What is revealed about your heart because of that fear? Is there an unresolved conflict in your life that stems from that fear? Did you have a bad experience? Perhaps there is a simple lack of trust in God over something outside of your control?

Take some time and try to specify what that fear is. Write it here: _____

_____

Now, re-read Psalm 27:1-3 (I used the ESV version of the Bible) and insert your fear into this paraphrased version of that passage:

The Lord is my light and my salvation — why should I be afraid of (_____)? The Lord is the strength of my life; protecting me from danger, so why should I be afraid of something like (_____)? When evil people come to devour me, when my enemies and foes (and _____) attack me, they will stumble and fall. Though a mighty army surrounds me, my heart will not be afraid. Even if I am surrounded on all sides and if I am attacked by (_____), I will remain confident.

Next, take a picture of the above and save it to your phone. Store it somewhere where you will see it often. Perhaps as your wallpaper, or maybe even print it out. Put it on your bathroom mirror or perhaps on your fridge. Repeat it as often as you need to throughout the day to be reminded of the glory of God and the work that he can do. Reflect on it throughout the week, and continually surrender your fear(s) to God through prayer.

PRAYER

Father, I admit, my fears have made decisions on my behalf. I have allowed them to have a bigger impact in my life than I would like to admit. I know You are bigger than any fear I may have. I surrender my fears to You now. My trust is in You alone, and I know that fear can be a result of lack of faith. I will not fear anything in creation, whilst I know the Creator. I pray You go before me this day, and give me an overwhelming peace that only You can give. I know You always have my best interest at heart, and I praise You for that. In Your name, Amen.

PRAYER
(write your own)

_____

_____

_____

_____

_____

_____

_____

_____

_____

Commute Encounters

From a Yard

SCRIPTURE
*1 Corinthians 12, Galatians 1:10,
Matthew 25:14-29, Luke 16:10*

Though I do drive through country backroads most of my commute, I do eventually reach the city. As I enter the city, I pass through an upscale neighborhood with gated communities. I can't help but look around and wonder how much money these people make. I take in their large houses and think how different it looks from my own neighborhood.

I see their large front yards full of rich green grass. They have impeccable landscaping with the most beautiful of flowers in bloom and not a weed in sight. My eyes scan over to their driveway, and I see the owner of the house in the driveway polishing off his Mustang.

I pull into work and see my coworkers in the parking lot. I can't help but think how much nicer and more "put together" they look than me. They definitely got more sleep than I did!

I settle into my desk at work and take a quick look at Facebook. I read about my friends' incredible vacations and trips, and wish I had the money and time to do the same. A little one makes it hard to travel these days.

Physical possessions aside, I know other individuals who are more patient and hospitable than me. Some have career opportunities that I desire, while others have personal characteristics that I envy.

Man, this is a dangerous game to play, isn't it? In one morning alone, I looked into the "yard" of another and coveted multiple times. Looking back and repeating the morning in my head, this is what I realized (bear with me as we re-walk through the previous paragraphs):

I pass through an upscale neighborhood with gated communities. Hmm. I wonder why it has to be gated? Have they had incidents that require the community to now be gated?

I can't help but look around and wonder how much money these people make. I take in their large houses and think how different it looks from my own neighborhood. My husband and I make more than enough money. We live comfortable lives and are well taken care of. Praise the Lord for stable careers!

I see their large front yards full of rich green grass. They have impeccable landscaping with the most beautiful of flowers in bloom and not a weed in sight. That must require a ton of time and work. I definitely don't have that kind of time, or even energy, especially now having a baby boy to tend to. I wonder if these homeowners are retirees, or have children of their own?

My eyes scan over to their driveway, and I see the owner of the house in the driveway polishing off his Mustang. I have my own brand-new SUV. How quickly I forget what I have been blessed with.

I pull into work and see my coworkers in the parking lot. I can't help but think how much nicer and more "put together" they look than me. They definitely got more sleep than I did! These aren't just coworkers; they are my friends! I am thrilled to see them, and get to spend the day with them. I hope got plenty of sleep last night, and are well rested to tackle their day ahead.

I settle into my desk at work and take a quick look at Facebook. I read about my friends' incredible vacations and trips, and wish I had the money and time to do the same. I do have the money and time; I just choose to prioritize differently these days. It's awesome that my friends can treat themselves to vacations and make those memories with their families. I can't wait until our family gets to do the same someday.

A little one makes it hard to travel these days. Yes, my baby boy. I am blessed to even have a child, when there are so many others who wrestle in this area. I am overwhelmingly blessed that the Lord gave us a child.

Physical possessions aside, I know other individuals who are more patient and hospitable than me. I have personally been blessed by the patience and hospitality of others. My family has been invited into our friends' homes and treated to game nights, wonderful meals, and good company.

Some have career opportunities that I desire, while others have personal characteristics that I envy. The Lord has placed you right where he wants you, Lindsay. You love what you do, and you're doing what you love.

Do you see it, reader? Do you see the change we need to make in our minds to re-evaluate and morph our perspective? Satan would love nothing more than for me to constantly live in a state of comparison, letting jealousy root and grow in my heart.

Scripture tells us that the church is one body, made up of many parts. These parts do not look alike, and yet they all perform vital tasks. Friends, amidst this diverse world, we *must* be united and put away this game of comparison. It is so incredibly dangerous, and tempts us to start looking at our friends as enemies.

It is true that others in this world will receive things that we never will. Some will have incredible opportunities and impressive abilities that you never will, and that's okay! At times like these, I lovingly remind myself that there are some people in this world who overwhelmingly desire the opportunities and abilities that I myself have. It is vital in this reshaping of our minds that we remember we will always have something that someone else desperately desires. This isn't to boost our own pride or value, but it is to simply remind ourselves that what we each have is enough in the eyes of the Lord. He has entrusted us with what we have, and we worship Him by honoring that.

You are uniquely designed just as you are, and you are uniquely gifted with exactly what you have. Focus your mind on the blessings in your life, and put away this game of comparison.

INVITE HIM IN

Imagine a world where comparison wasn't a thing. What do you suppose would happen if we chose to see the blessings and abilities of others and immediately rejoice, instead of wondering "what about me and mine?" Jesus doesn't call us to all be perfect and to all have good things. He calls us to follow Him. Start today by choosing to take a perspective of thanksgiving for what you have, and not an eagerness for wanting more. If we choose to use the gifts and abilities already entrusted to us, the Lord will surely use them for His glory and may even choose to multiply them.

Today, I challenge you to intentionally identify those things that the Lord has blessed you with. Take time right now and write down three unique things the Lord has entrusted to you. Now I don't mean the typical things like family, friends, pets, etc., but think of things that are unique to *you*. God has gifted *you* with things that He hasn't gifted to me, or maybe to anyone else. Take time to reflect on those unique blessings, and pray thanksgiving over them.

1. _____

2. _____

3. _____

PRAYER

Father, thank You for the things You have blessed me with in this worldly life. I am so sorry for not appreciating all of it as often as I should, and for coveting what is in my neighbor's yard. I ask that You give me a new sense of thankfulness today, and to increase in me the ability to rejoice with my brothers and sisters in their accomplishments. All good things come from You, Lord. Help me to keep that in the forefront of my heart when my mind tends to wander. Amen.

PRAYER
(write your own)

_____
_____
_____
_____
_____
_____
_____
_____
_____
_____

Commute Encounters

From a Mother

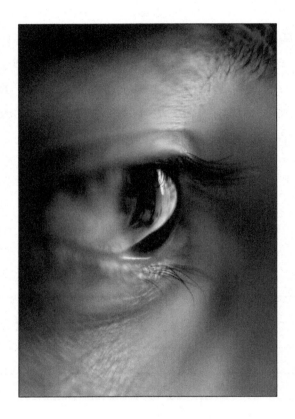

SCRIPTURE

Philippians 2:3-7, Galatians 5:16, Colossians 3:12-14, John 13:34-35

On some mornings, I must admit, I'm intentionally late for work. I mean - how can I not snuggle my baby boy just one more time before walking out the door? How can I not give my husband one last kiss? It's practically a mandatory obligation to top off my coffee cup too! I couldn't possibly survive the day without it.

Glancing at the kitchen clock one last time, I hustle to grab my bags and head out the door for work. If I drive just a smidge over the speed limit, then I'll be able to make up the difference in no time.

Fast forward a few minutes and I'm following behind a black sedan on a two-lane road. There's little to no opportunity to pass on this particular road, so I was quite stuck following this little car. It seemed like the driver was almost taunting me, somehow knowing that I was running late for work. They would seemingly speed up, and slow down again over and over.

I chuckled to myself and thought maybe this was my divine punishment for intentionally leaving late for work today. I do like to think God has a good sense of humor on some days.

This car and I eventually made our way onto a highway that turned into a four-lane road. I immediately got in the left lane and initiated my plan of pass and push (pass the car, push the speed limit).

Naturally, as soon as I began to pull up alongside the black sedan, they also sped up. In fact, it seemed like they were practically flooring it. The competitive nature in me took over. I gripped my steering wheel and decided that it was time to race.

I pushed down on the gas pedal even harder, while scanning the horizon for any police cars that may be nearby. Confirming their absence, I hit the gas pedal and eventually pulled up neck and neck with the black sedan.

Naturally, my instinct is to look over at the sedan driver and gloat. I resisted the temptation, but could feel the smirk form across my face. Instead, I look up and see a yellow traffic light appear up ahead of us.

Still traveling side by side, we both hit our brakes and rolled to a stop. Out of the corner of my eye, I see them throw their hands up in disbelief. Our race has been put on "pause" with no indication of a winner yet.

A little part of me snickers, assuming she must have come to the same realization that I did. We would now have the pleasure of awkwardly sitting right next to each other until this light turned green. Now the question is, who is going to look over at who first?

I decided I would be the brave one to make the first move, and I took a quick side-eye assessment of their car. The first thing I noticed was the graduation tassel hanging from their rearview window.

Great. I'm dealing with some teenager.

The second thing I noticed was the condition of the sedan. The paint was chipped off in a few places, and rust was claiming a home. The front had a couple dings and dents, but nothing to indicate teenage recklessness.

Keep your thoughts to yourself, Linz.

The third thing I noticed was their hand was up like a mini shield, blocking me from seeing their face.

I'd be embarrassed if I were them too. They were going to get smoked in that race!

It felt like time was crawling at a snail's pace as we waited for the light to turn green. I'd sneak glances over at the sedan every now and then, and finally, I saw them lower their hand.

The fourth thing I noticed in this encounter was when that hand had been lowered. Instead of the person being an unruly teenager, she was actually another young woman who had to have been about my age (early 30s). She had tears rolling down her cheeks and looked incredibly distraught.

The final thing I saw in this encounter was two little feet sticking out from a car seat in the back.

I felt a softball-sized lump develop in my throat; my own tears building up as well. Reader, if you've read my chapter "From a Grocery List", then you already know how tender my heart is for new moms.

I had a brief flashback to when she threw her hands up in the air, and realized that that wasn't about me. This mother couldn't care less about our "race". She cared about getting to where she (or her child) needed to be. Perhaps she was late for daycare, and therefore also late for work. Perhaps her child was ill, and she was in a panic trying to get them both to help and safety. For all I know, she just received tragic news about a family member and was rushing to make it somewhere in time.

I'll never know what exactly her situation was, but I had the clear realization that I was adding unnecessary fuel to her fire.

She was in distress, and I'm forcing her to "race". She's wiping tears, and I'm wearing a smirk. She's in over her head, and I'm heavy-footing my gas pedal.

My mama bear heart got the best of me here, and I felt so overwhelmed with guilt. In that moment, being on time for work wasn't so important anymore. The coffee that I claimed to require and desired so deeply wasn't so important anymore. Intentionally pushing the speed limit wasn't so important anymore, knowing that it wasn't just risking my own life, but also that of this mother and child.

I let out a deep breath and began to pray for this mother. I prayed that God would give her a peace and a comfort with whatever trial was in her path this morning. I prayed for the Lord to give her guidance and wisdom as she continued to navigate her drive. I prayed she would have people placed in her path that would serve as a better witness to her than I had.

The light turned green, and the mother began her journey again. I waited a few seconds before I took my foot off the brake and let it be clear to her that I wasn't interested in "racing" anymore.

I kept a slow pace, and watched her car fade farther off into the distance. I prayed over her and her child one last time as they were forever removed from my sight, but forever engrained on my heart.

I so desperately wish our interaction would have been different. Yet, I know that the Lord is bigger than me and will use that experience for His glory. At least, that has been my prayer. I also know full well that the Lord has and will continue to extend grace to me for my foolish actions and behavior; though that doesn't excuse my recklessness.

This encounter overwhelmed me with conviction. I may be the only Christian someone encounters in their life. Am I representing Jesus well?

INVITE HIM IN

Sometimes when we are chasing after our own sinful desires, we don't notice the ripple effect that we have on others. Every word we say and every action we take has an impact on another person or situation. If we're not careful, when we let our sinful flesh influence our behavior, we can subconsciously deny the well-being of another. Now imagine what the world would look like if we focused primarily on the well-being of others. What do you suppose it would look like? As new creations redeemed by Jesus, we are called to love each other, just as Christ loved us. Easier said than done on some occasions, but a commandment nonetheless.

Today, I challenge you to reflect on the last 24 hours of your life. Try to think of a specific instance from your day where your words or actions had a direct influence on another specific person; good or bad. Try to pick just one individual, if multiple were involved. Now, replay the scenario and relive it through the eyes of the person you selected. Was it a disagreement you had with your spouse or a parent? Maybe a conflict with your child or a coworker? Think of how your actions and words could have affected them. How could they have felt? What could they have carried away with them after that encounter? What lingering impact is there?

PRAYER

Father, forgive me for thinking of only me. You have called me to love others above myself, though I falter in this area on occasion. Soften my heart, and help me see others through Your eyes. Give me the strength and courage to sacrifice myself for the sake of others, whom I know You love just as dearly as You love me. Give me the eyes to see them as You see them – perfect, handcrafted creations of Your hands. Let love be my motivator, Lord. Give me the clarity to see the impact of my words and actions, and give me the tenderness to seek reconciliation where needed. Amen.

PRAYER
(write your own)

_____
_____
_____
_____
_____
_____
_____
_____
_____

Commute Encounters

From a Red Light

SCRIPTURE

1 Corinthians 1:10, 1 John 3:17-19, Philippians 2:2, 1 Corinthians 12:12-14, 1 John 4:19

With my position at work, there are some nights of the week where I don't leave for home until well after dark. There have been some nights in the past where I haven't gotten home until almost 11pm! That doesn't happen too often, but on those particular nights, I am certainly ready to be home.

One night in March of 2019, I was just getting back into town after a somewhat stressful day at work. I wanted nothing more than to be home where a hot shower and stretchy pants were calling my name.

I turned on to my darkened street when I saw a soft glow of a red light coming from a house on the corner. The homeowner had placed a lamp containing a red lightbulb in one of their main windows.

The next house had a mini streetlight in their front yard as décor, and they had replaced its default lightbulb with a red one. The next house also found their own way to display a red lightbulb, as did the next house and the next.

Here's some context: a couple months prior, in January of 2019, my hometown had experienced an absolute tragedy. Two of our city's beloved firefighters had been involved in an explosion while on a fire call at a local river terminal and transportation plant. One suffered terrible injuries, but thankfully survived. The other, a hometown boy who many knew, passed away due to the injuries he sustained. It was an awful day, and our little town was shaken to its core.

This was especially hard my family and me, as both my husband and my brother are also firefighters on that same fire station. In fact, my husband was on the same call when the explosion occurred, and he unfortunately witnessed things I wish his eyes never had to see. My brother played a role that day as well and had in fact gone to high school with the firefighter who lost his life. My heart broke for him, as I knew he was affected and hurt more than he had ever let on.

The events of that day were so significant, our city and the surrounding communities did everything imaginable to show support for the families and firefighter community. Many businesses put up signs of support in their windows. Some community members created apparel honoring the firefighter who lost his life, and donated all the proceeds to his wife and daughter that he left behind. Many people simply brought food and meals to the fire stations in the city.

All of these gestures were so unbelievably considerate, and the community felt united like never before. With all of these acts in motion, it became clear that not *everybody* could do such elaborate things to show support. It was then that someone in the community (I don't know who), brought up the suggestion of a simple, visual sign of united support for the firefighters and their families: red lightbulbs.

Red is the perfect color to use in remembering the firefighters. Red is the symbolic color for the firefighter brotherhood, which is also commonly referred to as the "thin red line". Most firetrucks are red, fire is symbolized with red, and many fire hydrants are red. Combining that with a common household item (such as a lightbulb), the red lightbulb idea emerged.

In our city's massive Facebook group, this community member shared their idea, and hundreds of people jumped on it. Soon, many stores were suddenly selling out of their red lightbulb supply. People were having to special order red lightbulbs online, or travel to other cities to purchase them.

The idea was for households in the community to replace their front door light with a red lightbulb. Some chose to use red Christmas lights to outline their windows, and others used red lawn décor. One automotive business in town lined up the front of their lot with all red vehicles to form their own "thin red line". A donut store a few cities over even created simple glazed donuts with a red line of frosting across the top, donating all their proceeds to the firefighters' families.

There are many more instances where this unity was on display, and it was such a touching thing to be a part of. My family felt overwhelming support, and I know the two families of the victims did as well. It was refreshing to have a renewed sense of hope in humanity; even if something so tragic had to happen to spur it on.

As I continued on my drive home, I couldn't help but reflect and remember all that the community had done in the previous months. Everyone had played a role, offering up whatever support they could give. Each gift looked different, but each was so vital in helping the families impacted and the community to recover. No gift was less or more than any of the others, and the heart behind the generous motions were the same.

No action or words could replace the loss of that dear firefighter, or take away the pain of the one who survived, but love was on full display.

I pulled into my driveway, and found my mind wandering to Scripture. Specifically, the passage describing the body of Christ having many members. Each member looks different and has unique functions, but the common goal is unity. The sense of togetherness and need for one another to succeed and thrive; to sustain and support. That passage in Scripture is referencing the body of Christ, but I couldn't help but notice the similarity between that and what the community was doing.

I stepped out my car as stood in silence in the driveway. I looked around my neighborhood, and spared a minute to take in the red lights scattered about. Breathing in the chilled air, my eyes turned to our own red light glowing in our front window. The only thought that seemed to consume my mind is this. We are one. We are united.

Man, thank you Jesus for giving us the gift of compassion and unity. We love, because he loved us first.

INVITE HIM IN

There are many instances where unity and oneness serve as an unstoppable force. We occasionally hear of marriage ceremonies containing the braiding of three chords. If you're a nature buff, you know that many animals travel in packs to ensure safety. Likewise, we see many instances in Scripture where numbers are considered incredibly valuable. Knowing that we have Christ and fellow believers on our side, we know that our church family is a strong and unbreakable one. Each of us serves our own role and can offer up our own unique things, but each serves as a necessary and beyond valuable member. Imagine the powerful things the Lord can do through us if unity and oneness is our goal.

Today, I challenge you to take a minute and reflect on yourself as a member of the body of Christ. What role do you view yourself as having? Do you know what your spiritual gifts are? Is oneness an observable thing to those on the outside looking in at your church family and community? These are some incredibly heavy things to think through, and I urge you to take the time to focus on them for the next several minutes. There are many free resources online to help you discover your spiritual gifts. Find one of those resources online now, and begin the process of discovering what your gift(s) is.

PRAYER

Father, thank You for the unity of the church. Thank You for the unity of Your people. We know that strength lies in numbers, and that You have enabled us to love on one another in that way. You uniquely shaped and created each one of us to serve a role, and I pray You reveal to us more and more each day what those giftings are. I pray You encourage us to use those gifts for Your glory, and to demonstrate Your love to those around us. We trust in You, God, and we submit and surrender all that we have to You. In Your precious name, Amen.

PRAYER
(write your own)

_____

_____

_____

_____

_____

_____

_____

_____

_____

Commute Encounters

From CDs

SCRIPTURE

Matthew 6:24, James 3:8-12, 2 Corinthians 5:17

Another Monday morning. The weekend flew by like it always does, and I'm once again getting into my car to depart for another work week. Typically, I would turn on my local Christian radio station to prepare my mind for the work day. However, I thought today I'd spice things up with a little bit of throwback music.

I opened my center console and dug around for an old CD case I knew I had stashed in there somewhere. Most of the discs were custom burned CDs I had made for myself back in my late teen/early college years. I decided I'd pick one at random and give it a listen.

After a couple moments of buffering, the rock/rap music began. A solid start, until the lyrics hit. I quickly recalled that this particular song was about clubbing, drinking, and sexual rebounds. Not typically a song I would listen to, but this band must have been very popular at the time.

The next song that came on had a dance feel to it, and was about how the word "love" means nothing. It emphasized that one-night stands were the way to go. The vocalists described themselves as serial daters, who were okay taking advantage of innocent bodies.

I cringed as the words poured out of my speakers, and I quickly hit my skip button.

The next song was about leaning on God during the hard times. How love calls us to turn to Christ when we feel broken, and alone. He is everything that we could ever need. This song was a breath of fresh air, and I smiled to myself.

The next song that came on described in graphic detail the joy of appreciating the bodies of the opposite sex. It contained cat calling, descriptions of well-endowed women, see through clothing and grinding.

Next was a song describing school shootings, suicide and sexual abuse.

The next song was about helping the lost get found. How we need to reach out to those around us and be witnesses for the love of Jesus. It was a song of pure hope, with an emphasis on outreach.

I could continue, but reader, do you see the problem here? Talk about one foot in the world and one foot in the church! Words can't describe how foolish I felt, as I found myself regularly hitting the "skip" button. I couldn't believe I had something so repulsive in my car, and I could practically feel the word "hypocrite" appearing on my forehead.

In college, I had deeply fooled myself into thinking I could boast Christ's name in one moment, then spill out vile in my very next breath through these lyrics. Friends, Scripture is clear that we cannot serve two masters. We cannot allow ourselves to think we can have it both ways. We are only fooling ourselves, and our childish instabilities will eventually lead to our spiritual demise.

As I listened on, occasionally I would hear a song that would remind me of a particular friend. Whether it be a song that we would jam out to together, or a song that they were especially fond of. This is where my biggest conviction would arise; while I was actively choosing to head down a sinful path, I probably took others along with me.

Even to this day I often think back to specific people in my past who trusted me, who I feel I messed up or misled. I've spent countless hours crying out to God on their behalf, *begging* with everything I had in me that the Lord would correct my wrong in their life. I've slowly been learning to let go of that burden, but I will never stop praying for them. Someday, maybe those particular people will read this chapter, and know that I am talking about them. Lord only knows. If that be the case and you are reading this, please, forgive me.

As I continued driving, the realization of my deep sinful lifestyle whilst in college continued to set in. I couldn't help but feel the tears well up, as I turned my head upward and cried out to God. Yes, the regret was in there, but more so, the strongest feeling that overtook me in this moment was thankfulness.

Thankfulness for his grace and mercy in my life. Thankfulness for the dangers he delivered me from during those lost college days. Thankfulness for the new life he has given me, in the ultimate act of redemption.

You see, when Jesus died on the cross in our place, he redeemed us by his blood. Once we have accepted him as Lord and Savior, and surrender our lives to him, he makes us a new creation. We get a new start in his name. For a broken sinner like me, that was the best thing I could have ever asked for.

I spent the rest of my drive working my way through all of the burned CDs I had in my car. If any of them had even one bad song on it, I moved it to a "garbage" pile, where they would await their playdate with my trashcan when I eventually got home.

Let me be clear - these CDs were made at least 10+ years ago. They are not recent, nor have I listened to any of those songs in a long, long time. However, I was a self-proclaiming "Christian" when I did make them. My allegiance was torn between God and the world.

That said, I am so incredibly thankful I rediscovered Christ right after college graduation. I knew the gospel before that day, but it wasn't something I let lead my life in the past. I had a "reunion" of sorts, which you'll read more about in a later chapter. That day (July 7, 2011), I chose to make Jesus the Lord of my life. I submitted everything and my all to Him and His way. Even now as I sit here writing this, I can't help but look back to where I was and where I am now. I've come so ridiculously far, and I have the Lord to thank for that.

Friends, simply put, my life is the definition of grace. I do not deserve to be where I am, and yet, the Lord is merciful. So much could have happened to me in college that didn't, and I can only explain it as simply grace from God. I have kept a lot of my college experience private, as it is extremely personal, graphic, and embarrassing. However, if you continue to read on, I may offer a bit more insight in a later chapter.

Some of my experiences caused me to seek out professional counseling. Some caused my parents true heartache, despair, tears, anger, and most importantly, forgiveness. Some experiences caused friends to abandon me or boyfriends to break up with me. Some caused permanent scarring (both physically and emotionally) thanks to the evil actions of other individuals; many of which, still haunt me to this day.

Some of you knew me back then and are probably silently agreeing with me that yeah, she's seen some stuff. She's done some stuff. I prayerfully hope that today, you can see now how my life has transformed thanks to Jesus. Similarly, some of you may have met me only in recent years and can't possibly believe some of these details in my journey. I pray that's the case, and that it's clear my old life is long gone.

I am a new creation.

INVITE HIM IN

Once you have turned over your life over the Lord, Scripture calls you a new creation. How cool is that! The old life is gone, and your new life in Jesus has come. Admittingly, sometimes it can be hard to turn from and forget about your old life. If you struggle with that, I urge you to lean on Jesus. Take some time and ask the Lord to give you an unwavering strength to leave that life far behind you. Jesus doesn't judge you for what you've said or done. He doesn't hold it against you. He already conquered death and took the burden of sin for you – you can trust him with your old baggage too.

Today, I challenge you to take some honest time to evaluate the life you're living. Are there areas in your life where you are still displaying the "you" of the past? Look at your daily activities, routines, hobbies, words, *whatever* it may be where a version of the former you may linger. If you struggle to find it, then that's incredible. I'm so proud of you for fully embracing being the new creation in Christ that you are. It's not always easy to do that – stay strong! If you *have* found it, then I am also proud of you. Identifying that in our lives can be difficult or shameful. Have some intentional quiet time right now to surrender those things up to God.

PRAYER

Dear Jesus, thank You for paying the ultimate price for me and for reclaiming me as Your own. Thank You for loving me enough to sacrifice Yourself in my place and forgiving me for my sins. I ask, Lord, that You help me become more like You every day. Refine me. Sharpen me. Break me. Restore me. Lord, I pray for strength to leave the past behind, and only look forward. I ask for the endurance to continue progressing, through all that that may entail for me. I trust You, Father. I am Yours. I am new. Thank you. Amen.

PRAYER
(write your own)

_____

_____

_____

_____

_____

_____

_____

_____

_____

Commute Encounters

From a Song

SCRIPTURE

*2 Timothy 3:16-17, Ezekiel 36:26, Proverbs 31:8-9,
Ephesians 5:11, James 4:17, Matthew 10:22*

As an ever-learning follower of Jesus, I occasionally struggle with not speaking up and defending biblical teachings when the moment arises. I get in my own head being concerned about my reputation and image, and also wondering if I will be able to handle the confrontation. I worry that the exchange will be overheard or that maybe I'll get blasted on social media. The vast majority of the time, I find myself not speaking up for one of these five reasons:

1. I don't want to upset them or start a fight
2. I don't really know them that well
3. It's not my business
4. Someone else will say something
5. I don't want others to see/hear our exchange

This day in May of 2020, a particular issue has been on my mind and it has been eating away at me. I had been on social media this morning, and saw a particular friend boasting out in support of this topic. This topic has been a hot one to discuss in society lately, ever since the names Roe and Wade became familiarized in households. I've shared my stance on this topic with companions who I know will stand alongside me; however, when it comes to others who I know support this topic, I've typically chosen to sit on the sidelines and lay an egg.

I was letting the words and harsh comments I had read on social media earlier that morning bounce around in my head. The stance that she took bothered me severely, but I still had chosen to not engage. As God sometimes chooses to do, he pulled a God-thing on me this morning. While driving to work, I heard the song "Do Something" by artist Matthew West come on the radio. It immediately made my stomach churn out of guilt and conviction.

Wait – time out. Have you heard that song, reader? If not, spare five minutes of your life and look it up on YouTube right now.

No, I'm serious. Go do it. I'll wait.

Have you done it yet?

Okay, great!

Now that we are all familiarized with the song, I imagine you have pieced together where this chapter is going. I have no desire to dive deep into the specific hot topic that I alluded at earlier, though it does lead me to the reminder the Lord graced upon me this morning. Fellow Bible believers, in a gentle, loving, and grace-filled manner, we <u>must</u> speak up. We are advocates for the Lord.

We are not needed, but we have been chosen to represent Him and progress His Kingdom. When we encounter those who knowingly (or even unknowingly) speak out against God's commands in Scripture, we have to do something.

It can be wildly intimidating to initiate that conversation with someone, but if we don't at least try, who will? Sometimes this means having a difficult conversation with a parent, spouse or close friend. Sometimes it means a brother or sister in Christ, or even a boss or coworker. Whatever the case may be, it probably won't always be an easy conversation to have. Unfortunately, we sinful humans tend to have a little pride issue and we don't like being wrong. However, that isn't enough reason to stand idly by on the sidelines. As the song implies, we're never going to change the world by standing still.

I let out a deep breath as I continued to let the lyrics of that song wash over me on this morning. The level of conviction that I felt was more than enough for me to know I had to speak up about this topic. At this time, I was four months pregnant with my firstborn, and the idea that people don't see him as valuable as me absolutely crushes my heart. I felt goosebumps form on my arm, as I knew that I would have to have a difficult conversation with a friend later on that evening.

I had no idea how it would go, but I didn't have a very good feeling about it. She has a very strong foundation in her beliefs, and while I don't aim to try to knock her down, I know I must speak up and out for those who can't speak for themselves.

Readers, I would love to let you know how this bit of encounter/story ends for me, but unfortunately, I don't have the conclusion yet. With particularly heavy topics such as this, one conversation won't do justice. This will certainly be an ongoing thing, especially with politics being the focus this year (in the midst of the COVID-19 pandemic).

One thing I do want to leave you with though, is that ultimately, only God can change a heart. We can certainly play a role and submit ourselves before God to be used at His discretion and wisdom, but ultimately, the war is His. That is both a humbling reminder, but also a beautiful promise.

INVITE HIM IN

Scripture tells us that by being a follower of Jesus, we are an enemy of the world. This becomes evidently true when we seek to speak out biblically when it comes to hot topics in society. Imagine what would happen if all of the Bible believing people in our country were to step into the ring of endless debate and speak out in Jesus' name. Goodness, do I pray for that. I pray that we can all be more bold and more fearless. I pray that the Lord will continue to convict us, and sharpen us in both preparation and outcome. It won't be an enjoyable process, but the Kingdom is worth it.

Today, I challenge you to select one potential hot topic in society that you are or could be passionate about. I have made my fairly clear, but here are a few other ideas: immigration, government mandates, LGBT rights, war, gun control, animal rights. Select one of them, and write it here: _____

Now, turn to Scripture and do some research. Find what God says about that topic, or what could be relevant to that topic. Find at least three different passages that could help morph your opinion, or further solidify it. Pray over it, and ask the Lord to give you guidance on how to start beneficial conversation over your topic.

PRAYER

Lord, we live in a world full of controversy and differing sides and opinions. Everyone wants to have a voice, but the only voice that we need to seek out and rest in is Yours. I pray You give me the wisdom to discern the different voices I hear all around me, and to hone in on Yours alone. Give me the strength to echo Your voice into the lives of those around me. Help me to have the patience and clarity to accurately reflect Your scriptural stance on issues. Lord, give our nation a soft and teachable heart. Help us to see things as You see them, and to love people as You love people. Amen.

PRAYER
(write your own)

_____
_____
_____
_____
_____
_____
_____
_____

Commute Encounters

From a Scar

SCRIPTURE
Proverbs 3:5-6, Psalm 28:7, Jeremiah 29:11

On my drive home after work one evening, I found myself being incredibly judgmental of my own body. As I was driving, I had one hand on the steering wheel and the other hand on my lower abdomen; right over the scar from my cesarean section (c-section). I gained this scar only five(ish) months ago, after having given birth to my first child.

I lifted my shirt up ever so slightly, and let my fingers trace over the scar. I ran my fingertips over it, going back and forth, and back and forth. I let out a small breath and smiled as my mind went to my sweet baby boy.

My fingertips strayed from my precious scar, and moved to the bulge of skin that resided next door. I poked at it and squeezed it. It surrounded my scar completely. The smile faded from my face as no matter how I adjusted and contorted my body, the bulge remained. I felt the betrayal of a single tear escape as I set my shirt back down, and let my hand rejoin the other on the steering wheel.

When I set out to write this book, I assumed every chapter would be based on an encounter with other people or nature; I never thought the encounter would be with my own body and mentality.

Motherhood is something I never knew I needed. Anyone who knew me in my late teens/early adult years knew that I never wanted to get married or have kids. It was a declaration that I clung to, and I would boast it often. I simply didn't think I'd live that long, having high doubt in God's plans for my life.

Yet, take me back to October 26, 2020. My husband and I in a still hospital room. The doctors and nurses were looking at one another, and the clock, as I was approaching 4.5 hours of labor pushing. My son had become "stuck" as a result of being positioned face up when I went into labor. I was feeling extremely tired and overwhelmed, and if I'm being honest, I also felt incredibly defeated.

The doctor had been suggesting I have a c-section for the last two hours, but I had insisted on still aiming for a natural birth. The time had come for a change of plans, and everyone in the room knew it. I looked over at my husband, his concerned eyes already locked on mine.

There was no need to risk my life or that of my son's, so with fear hidden behind an exhausted smile, I nodded to the staff and a c-section was scheduled. It would be another two hours before the c-section actually happened, due to a shift change. I was in extreme pain during that waiting time, and a part of me was full of heavy regret.

The procedure itself was quite painless. My body gave out to exhaustion, and I slept through almost the whole thing. The only part I vividly remember about the experience was the anesthesiologist soothing me, running her fingers across my head. It was incredibly comforting, and my physical and mental self simply couldn't resist falling asleep.

That is, until I woke up to the precious sound of a baby cry. It took me a brief second to regain full consciousness and remember where I was, but goodness, did I immediately know I was right where I was meant to be. I was meant to be a mother. I was meant to be in this moment with my husband, as we welcomed our little one into the world. There's no doubt in my mind that the Lord had serious plans for my life, my husband's life, and this new life in my son.

When I finally got to hold him in my arms for the first time, my world was absolutely rocked. I looked over at my husband, as he offered me a sweet smile from behind his sleepy eyes. Taking in the reality of them both being mine, I was very humbled that the Lord had decided to bless me in this way that I swore I never, ever needed. I was so incredibly wrong with my "no husband, no kids" declaration, and praise Jesus for that! There was no feeling like looking down at this precious baby boy and getting to say "Hello Samuel" for the very first time.

I brought myself back to the present day, and loosened my grip on the steering wheel. My eyes scanned my surroundings, and finally rested on the sight of a herd of cattle and their offspring. The mothers grazed peacefully, while the little ones scampered about. Have you ever seen a calf attempt to run and jump in the midst of its playing? It is quite the sight!

I smiled and let my right hand drop once again and rest on my lower abdomen. Knowing where to go, my fingertips once again began to trace my c-section scar. That beautiful, priceless, little five-inch scar, that many women in this world would kill for. My mind was all over the place, as it typically has been since I became a wife and mother.

My mind went back to my beautiful son, and his projectile pees. They make me laugh every single time. My mind went to all of the cards I received at my baby showers, encouraging me and assuring me into motherhood.

My mind went to my husband, who lets me sleep at 2am, as he gets up to tend to the crying baby first.

My mind went to all of my dear friends and family, who I know have lifted me up in prayer countless times.

I wiped away that first tear of betrayal, as more tears of love and thankfulness followed. I smiled as I could feel them run down my cheeks, and I did nothing to stop them. I turned my eyes skyward and thanked the Lord for continually proving to me that His plans are more than enough, and always better than mine.

This scar has changed my life forever, and my body will never be the same ...and that's okay. While I may wrestle with that concept on occasion, I remind myself that it is worth it and I wouldn't change it for anything.

There's hope and healing in the story of my scar.
There's hope and healing in all of our scars.
Jesus proved that for us already, with the story of His scars.

INVITE HIM IN

Scripture has shown us time and time again that trusting the Lord is essential. The Creator of all the universe, and all that we know, loves us with every ounce of His being. With a love that big and endless, how could we choose not to trust His plan for our lives? We won't always understand it – in fact, we rarely will – but it's good.

One of the most popular bible verses used for encouragement is also one that is one (usually) taken out of context. It is a verse that promises hope for our lives, and promises that the Lord has great plans for us; that verse being Jeremiah 29:11. It's a verse I hold close to my heart, but it is a verse I had to research and dwell on deeply in order to understand and value it properly.

Today, I challenge you to dig deeper into that verse for yourself. Don't read just that verse, but read the full chapter. Strive to gain an understanding of the context and situation. You may have to do a little research on the internet to fully comprehend the scenario, and that is okay! Take your time. Once you have a good understanding of the passage and the context behind it, then fill in the blanks on the next page.

Did you *actually* go back and look into the context?
Yes _____ No _____ (okay, well go do it right now!)

Who is God speaking to? _____

Who is this verse about? _____

Where are they? _____

What just happened to them? _____

_____

_____

What does this promise from God show about his character? List 3 different things:

    1. _____

    2. _____

    3. _____

What does this mean for us today? _____

_____

_____

PRAYER

Father God, thank You for loving me enough to send Your Son to die in my place. Thank You for loving me enough to want what is best for me. Thank You for having a plan for my life, even if I can't always see it or understand it. I place my full trust in You, and the path that You have prepared for me. I know You are a good God, and I commit my uncertainty to You. I pray You cast it away from me, as I continually learn to simply trust the work that You are doing in my life. Thank You for the example You give in the book of Jeremiah, so that we can learn more and more about Your character and who You are. Lord, we don't deserve the plans You have for us; but thank You for continually choosing to redeem us. Amen.

PRAYER
(write your own)

_____

_____

_____

_____

_____

_____

_____

Commute Encounters

From Poop

SCRIPTURE

Proverbs 13:10, Matthew 25:14-30, Isaiah 2:11a, Proverbs 12:15, Proverbs 1:5, Proverbs 16:18

The excitement that comes with engagement and being a fiancé is like no other. I had met my now-husband in the summer of 2016 through our church, and I was instantly drawn to him. In fact, I had told a friend seconds after meeting him (and he had walked away) that I would marry him someday.

He was serving as a volunteer leader in the Student Ministry, and I had just been hired on to work full-time at the church as an Administrative Assistant in the Student Ministry. Naturally, our paths eventually crossed, and we met face to face. We ended up dating only 2 months later, and then within another 2 years, he was on one knee asking me for my hand in marriage.

I was so giddy and excited, and I immediately began planning our future in my head. I dreamed of what our lives would look like and I thanked the Lord for creating the perfect love story for us. It was one that only He could have orchestrated.

Following our engagement, I left my studio apartment and moved into my parent's home. Once we got married, I would then move into his house and we would begin our story as The Jacobsens.

Those 5 months of engagement is when my longer work commute began. It would take me 30 minutes to arrive at the church from my parent's home, and 45 minutes from Jeremiah's house. It wasn't something I was particularly excited about, but my desire to continue working in ministry far outweighed the drag of the commute. The only worry I had was driving in the winter, as my current vehicle was an older SUV with two-wheel drive. Knowing and sharing this concern, my fiancé decided it was time to update my vehicle.

After one trip to a local dealership, I was driving off the lot with a brand new 2018 Ford Escape with only 14 miles on it. It was the first time I've ever had a vehicle that wasn't at least 10 years old, and the power I felt when I gripped the steering wheel was exhilarating! I'm far from an adrenaline junkie, but there's just something special about a new car.

My fiancé warned me to take good care of it, and don't let the excitement of having a new vehicle cloud my judgement. Of course, I told him it wouldn't. I've always been a sharp driver who is aware of my surroundings. I've never been in an accident nor have I ever received a moving violation ticket of any sort. I was good to go!

In those first couple of weeks of driving my new SUV (named Lucy), I was having an absolute blast! I was zooming through the neighborhood, windows down and music blasting. I was passing everybody I possibly could on the highway with my sunglasses on, and music blaring. Yeah, I was *that* person.

Now, Iowa is a fairly tame and quiet state. We have a lot of fields growing all sorts of produce, and we have plenty of country farmland spread throughout the rural area. You can't go very far in the country without seeing horses, cows, goats, alpacas, pigs, and plenty more. Green John Deere farm equipment is ever populous, and is a staple of any large farm. While all of the large equipment these farmers have is quite impressive, most of it is also quite slow moving.

One early morning in September, I was cruising through the countryside on my way to work, as usual. There was a light mist hovering over the barren cornfields, and a certain crispness was in the air. It was a gorgeous morning, and nothing was going to slow me down. At least, not until I got stuck on a long country road behind a tractor pulling a large high-walled trailer.

It wasn't too big of a deal, but it did put a slight damper on my morning mood. The particular road we were driving on was full of twists and turns with few opportunities to pass, but I viewed that more as a challenge. I kept an eye out for an open window in which I could pass up this farm boy and his tractor getup, and tailgated as closely as I could. My souped-up SUV could accelerate pretty quickly; all I needed was a chance.

Unfortunately for me, the chance never happened. While my eyes were looking down the road, I stopped paying attention to what was right in front of me. I didn't notice the bumps and holes in the road, nor the content of the tractor's trailer sloshing around as a result.

One large pothole later, a good portion of the trailer's contents dumped out of the back and landed right in my path. My eyes turned towards it a second too late, and I found myself plowing through a giant pile of manure.

Visualize that for a second, will you? My beautiful, shiny, silver SUV – now covered on the frontside with brown liquidation of the cows. The smell was overpowering and my gag-reflex was on overdrive. Lucky for me, the tractor pulled off onto a property, and I was free to continue my commute cruise. I had the absolute joy of finishing the last 25-minute drive to work with the scent of poop wafting through my vents.

When I got to work, I went out to assess the front of my vehicle. Fortunately, there was no damage to anything other than my pride; though the wheels did have a nice, thick, brown layer caked onto them. I shared my encounter with a couple coworkers who found it to be quite hilarious. If I'm honest, I did too. My husband on the other hand, was a little less than pleased, but still lovingly teases me about it, even years later.

Though this encounter was a bit unpleasurable, it was ultimately harmless. My vehicle was eventually cleaned, and now it is just a funny memory. However, it did stir in me a new definition of the word "trust". This vehicle was entrusted to me, and I was to ensure that it was well taken care of. My husband and I both knew the value of this new SUV, and I was trusted to make sure that it was treated with high value. This means making sure my driving skills and awareness are exceedingly high, my distractions are non-existent, and that my decision-making was on point.

In regards to the tractor, I had let my selfish ambition cloud my judgement, and I ultimately paid a consequence. Fortunately for me, that consequence was minor and didn't result in somebody getting seriously injured.

My sinful pride over my new vehicle gave me an unrealistic image of power, letting me think that I was quite invincible. It also prodded me to think that the roadway belonged to me, and nobody else. That, my friends, is a very dangerous way to think, and ultimately, the Lord won't hesitate to humble it.

I would love to tell you that I haven't had any more gross encounters on the roadway with my vehicle, but you'll find out more about that in another chapter.

Stay tuned.

INVITE HIM IN

Scripture makes a clear stance on the danger of pride, and to those who refuse wise counsel. In fact, the Bible even goes so far to say that "pride goes before destruction" in Proverbs 16:18. It's a simple statement, but the result of not listening to it can be a heavy one. The Lord loves and will use a soft, teachable heart. If we humble ourselves and live a life embracing wisdom and guidance, imagine what the Lord could do through us! Imagine what the Lord could do through the church!

Today, I challenge you to reflect on those in the Bible who displayed a humble spirit, and were selected by God to progress His great plan due to their meekness. List three individuals below, and identify two ways they displayed their humility.

Name: _____
   1. _____
   2. _____
Name: _____
   1. _____
   2. _____
Name: _____
   1. _____
   2. _____

PRAYER

Father, I come before You today with a heart eager for humility. I know You use the weak to further Your great plan, and Lord, I want nothing more than to be used by You. Thank You for giving me the ability to be teachable. I pray that You place individuals in my life who will guide me in wise, scripturally-based counsel. I pray You give me the softness to seek out the wise when I feel at a loss. Lord, I know pride is a dangerous trait, and I pray You do an incredible work in me today. I want my life to be a shining example of You, always. Amen.

PRAYER
(write your own)

_____
_____
_____
_____
_____
_____
_____
_____

Commute Encounters

From a Dream

SCRIPTURE

*Psalm 86:5, Psalm 103:12, 2 Corinthians 5:17,
Philippians 1:6*

I grew up in an incredibly loving home. My mother, father, older brother and I all got along well, and had made many memories together over the years. Like every family, we had our fair share of ups and downs and arguments. Nevertheless, my family was and still is a close one.

All that to say, that eventually the time came when I graduated from high school and was getting ready to embark on my first experience away from home in college. I had the absolute privilege to attend the University of Dubuque, where I had some of the best times of my life. I was a Resident Assistant and a varsity tennis player. I had mostly good grades, and had made countless friends through classes, clubs, and even parties.

College was one of the best experiences of my life, but I also had my fair share of rough times. I made a few regretful decisions, and I put myself in some dangerous situations. Unfortunately, a couple of those dangers came to fruition and I ended up experiencing some immensely traumatizing events. I was left with severe emotional scarring that I was convinced I had no escape from ...or so I thought.

You read earlier in my "From CDs" chapter, that I had a reunion with Jesus after college graduation. Let me clarify what I mean by "reunion".

Growing up, my family discovered church and faith together. When my brother and I were young, my parents were invited to church from some family friends. It took a good bit of time for all 4 of us to be fully on board, but we eventually got there. My brother and I got involved in youth group where we were faithfully taught from Scripture, and given authentic life application. I will never forget those who impacted my life in those years. If you're reading this, thank you.

My parents and brother all got baptized during this faith exploration and time of learning, yet I had resisted and refused, even though I claimed to have had made a decision for Christ. I understood what I was being taught about the gospel, but for an unknown reason, I was struggling to embrace it. I knew plenty of the basics of who Jesus was and what a Christian life was supposed to look like, yet a part of me still hesitated.

I had strayed from my faith slightly in high school when I was influenced and then personally chose to pursue a sinful encounter. Yet, the name of Jesus lingered in the back of my mind. That lingering continued as I moved away to college. Even when I found myself making poor choices and being in some foolish situations, the name of Jesus was *always* in the back of my mind.

In those four years of school, I had partaken in some of the most reckless, stupid things that I am still incredibly embarrassed of. I will never glorify sin by going deep into discussion and "bragging" on what I got away with, but I do bring up the following things with a point. Brace yourself, mom and dad!

Though I can't recall what exact years these things took place, I did partake in the following: underage drinking, petty theft, driving under the influence, public intoxication, physically running from cops, a field sobriety test, sexual relationships (though maintaining my virginity), a near rape experience, a couple of failed classes. There's probably more, but I think perhaps I have made my point.

The point being this, readers: I was a lost, confused, foolish girl living immersed in the habits of the world, and yet Jesus still showed up and did a work that only He can do. He intervened and saved my life. That, dear reader, is what we call "grace".

It wasn't until after college graduation that I fully understood what God's grace meant. Here I was, living an ugly life, and yet He chose to spare me from the worst of those sinful things that I had been so deeply entrenched with. He snagged me from the jaws of ultimate danger, even though I didn't deserve rescuing. He showed me undeserved favor at my lowest point. He redeemed me and forgave me, and called me HIS. That, dear reader, is grace defined.

With all of those things I experienced, in all honesty, I shouldn't be where I am today. I probably should have ended up being expelled from school, or in jail, or perhaps not being on this earth anymore. Yet, here I am. I am alive, living a life that I never knew I could have. That, dear reader, is grace on display.

Fast forward several years, and I have put those sinful things behind me. I have surrounded myself with a solid Jesus-loving community, who are deeply rooted in their foundation of the faith. I have gotten involved in my church, and I keep my eyes looking onward and upward for whatever it is that the Lord may have in store for me next.

However, one lesson I have learned over the years is this: even when we make the best decision of our lives in accepting Jesus, that doesn't mean that Satan will give up on claiming us. We must continually be on guard, and remember that we are surrounded by spiritual warfare. My experience with spiritual warfare typically manifests itself in the form of dreams.

On one particular fall morning, I had one of those dreams and it shook me to my core. The dream forced me to relive one of those traumatizing experiences from college that I hoped to never think of again. It woke me up in the middle of the night with my heart racing, and my body drenched in sweat. I tossed and turned as I tried to fall back asleep, but I couldn't stop thinking about the dream. It felt so real.

I got in my car that morning and cranked up some worship music as loud as my ears could tolerate and sang my heart out, but I couldn't shake the dream. I prayed on and off throughout the drive, but I couldn't shake the dream. I cried out to God mentally throughout the day, but the vivid imagery wouldn't go away. Everything I tried had failed. The dream lingered with me all day.

Have you ever experienced that? A time where you felt so weighed down and haunted by your past that it seemed like your current life was at a permanent standstill? That day felt like a total loss, and I accepted defeat. I decided the best thing I could do for myself and those around me was to put my headphones in, listen to some Christian music, and just keep to myself for the rest of the day.

Now let me tell you something; God can use the simplest of things to teach a lesson. My day took a 180 degree turn when I heard a song come on the radio by one of my favorite Christian artists: "Prodigal" by Sidewalk Prophets. The two ideas within that song that resonated with me on this particular day were this:

Nights will come when we hear whispers of the past, but we can't let them linger. We are covered in grace, and we can't forget that when we are weak, the Lord is very strong.

Whatever we may have done, wherever we may have been, it's simply a page in our book, but the book isn't finished yet.

As those words echoed through my ears, I could feel the burden on my shoulders begin to lift. The Lord had orchestrated for the truths in that song to come at the absolute best time. I am not my past, nor is my story finished. The whispers may come and linger through the night, but my God is stronger. A dream is just a dream, and it can't rule over me.

As I shared earlier in this chapter, my life looks vastly different now than it did back in college. I have been overwhelmed by the demonstration of the Lord's grace and mercy in my life, and my mind no longer dwells on the sins of the past. This doesn't mean that hard days and hard times won't come – they certainly will – but with the help of the Holy Spirit, I can train my mind to focus primarily on God's truth.

I could choose to dwell on or run from the bad memories, but I will choose to learn from it instead. Thanks, Rafiki.

INVITE HIM IN

When we dwell on our former selves, it can be very easy for us to lose sight of the victory of the cross. Our weak, finite selves may struggle to move on from our past sins, but we must display a willingness to crucify them, not coddle them. A crucified enemy may still spit threats from its cross, but it no longer has true power over us. The power of Jesus in our lives will triumph endlessly, and we must cling to that truth. Keep your eyes on the victory of the cross; it is Satan's greatest fear.

Today, I challenge you to take some time glorifying God, specifically by acknowledging His grace and mercy in your life. We all have things in our past that the Lord has delivered us from. Some may still be a struggle; some we may have complete recovery from. Whichever the case, God deserves endless recognition for the work He has done and is still doing. Think of one specific thing, and spend some time in prayer. Use these three prompts to guide your quiet time:

1. Thanksgiving – for the progress that has been made
2. Grace – the gift we don't deserve, but still receive
3. Redemption – we are a work in progress, which Christ promises to complete

PRAYER

Jesus, forgive me for taking my eyes off of the cross. Even if it was only for a second, I know I can't let my eyes turn elsewhere. My sins and past no longer define me. You have claimed me; I am Yours. Lord, help solidify that fact in my mind. Deeply engrain it on my heart. Strengthen and renew my mind in a healing way that only You can accomplish. I ask that You give me the strength to let go of the things of yesterday, and to cling to Your promises of tomorrow. I love You, Lord. Thank You for creating a new person in me through Your son, Jesus. Amen.

PRAYER
(write your own)

Commute Encounters

From a Deer

SCRIPTURE
Proverbs 4:25-27, 2 Thessalonians 3:11-13, Luke 6:42

Most of the time, I get to enjoy a relatively peaceful, quiet work commute. The morning typically consists of a beautiful orange and pink sunrise above the cornfields, and the sunset is one that only God could create. Unless there's a storm in the forecast, I never have complaints about my restful work drive.

One of the main reasons I find it so restful is the regularity of it. I always know when to expect the sunrise and sunset. I know every twist and turn in the country roads, and the movement of the cornfields. I know the farmers routines and I see the same chores being performed each morning.

I'm sure many of you have experienced the "white noise" effect of a commute. You're so used to the same route and same routine, that you find yourself spacing out during your drive. Suddenly, you're at your destination and think "when did I get here!?" Your body went into auto-pilot mode, and you can't even recall consciously making the starts, stops, and turns that you did. Sometimes it can be a little worrisome when you realize you went through the "white noise" routine, but most times we don't think anything of it. At least, that is what I believed, until one night in the fall of 2018.

With having recently experienced the yearly time change, my night drive home was even darker than usual. The visual familiarity I had the month before took on a darker shade, but it was still familiar all the same. I slipped into my vehicle, left the church parking lot, and headed off into the country roads.

Although the majority of my drive consists of country and cornfields, there is only one particular road that I anticipate encountering wildlife. If you've read the chapter "From Poop", then you'll have an idea of what this road is like, and my "fond" memories of it.

This bluff road is a winding road with multiple farms on both sides. There are also patches of wilderness and trees tucked in between the farm homes, as if nature is trying to reclaim its original ownership. I typically don't think much of these patches of trees, but it does keep me on my toes when the occasional fox or raccoon runs out in front of me.

Even still, it is all a part of my regular routine, and I welcome it. I was about halfway down this particular road when I saw two pairs of headlights parked along my side of the shoulder. I still had a distance to go before I met them, but my curiosity was instantly peaked.

Was one of them having car trouble? Did they get into some sort of accident? Did one of them hit something? Are they just friends stopping to chat with one another? The questions raced through my mind, and I could feel my neck becoming more rubber-like by the second.

I did what any good driver would do, and I shifted over into the oncoming traffic lane, to allow them some additional safe space. No other cars were coming, so I felt perfectly safe taking my eyes off the road and turning to look at these two cars and their passengers as I drove by.

That's when I felt the large *thump* of my car as I hit what felt like a massive speedbump. My eyes suddenly shot forward again, but I saw no signs of anything that I may of hit. Out of sheer embarrassment, thinking I probably hit a turtle or something, I kept on driving. I am sure the owners of those two vehicles saw and/or heard what I just did, but there was no way I was stopping.

I accelerated, with the goal of putting as much distance between me and that *thump* as fast as possible. It felt like I was in a state of shock as I look back on it now and realize how irresponsible that was of me! For all I know,

I could have hit a person, or a pet, or who knows what; but instead, I took off like a coward.

It wasn't until about 20 minutes later when I pulled into my parent's driveway that I dared to step out of my car and investigate the front. Apparently, I had been so in shock with what had just happened that I had subconsciously decided to drive to their house instead of my own. That darn auto-pilot had struck again.

As I stepped out of my vehicle and made my way around to the front, I had only the streetlight across the road to make out the blood smeared across the hood of my car. My stomach dropped as I began to make out more red streaks and splatters on my tires, rims, and headlights. I ran inside their house to grab a flashlight, briefly filling my dad in on the situation.

With the flashlights help, I was now also able to see little tufts of brown and white fur stuck all over my car. There also appeared to be some guts (and other unmentionable gunk) stuck to the underside of my wheel wells. It was honestly one of the most disgusting things I have seen, but somehow, no damage was done to my vehicle.

After recounting the whole story to my dad, we had come to the conclusion that one of those two vehicles on the shoulder of the road had hit the deer, and the second vehicle had probably stopped to assist.

The deer may have still been alive whilst laying on the road when I came along and gave it a second helping, but that's a detail we will never know; nor need to know. Why did I choose to include that little sad visual portion here? I don't know. Every good story needs a little extra drama I suppose...

or maybe I should stop writing past 2am? Whoops.

I couldn't help but mentally kick myself as I realized this whole incident happened because I felt the need to rubberneck. If I had done what any driver should do and simply give them space while keeping my eyes on the roadway, I could have avoided this headache for myself. Now dear oh deer, did I pay the price this time!

I thanked my dad for his help, and headed off to the nearest carwash. Man, was my husband going to have a heyday teasing me about this one!

INVITE HIM IN

It can be very easy for us to look into the affairs of others, while ignoring what's going on in our own lane. Our curious minds are susceptible to wander into dangerous territory, and we must know how to navigate it. Scripture warns us to keep our eyes forward and our pathways straight. We are charged to do good work and to avoid idleness. Putting these two ideas together, we end up with a follower of Jesus who has the mindset that the Lord is doing a good work in all of our lives, and we should let that work continue without our selfish intervention driven by self-entitlement. This isn't to say we are to stay idle when a brother or sister in Christ is in danger or in need of help, but we should seek wisdom and pray for discernment before inserting ourselves into a situation.

Today, I challenge you to think on ways you can reframe your mind for when you are tempted to insert yourself into a situation. Does your motivation need to be checked? Are you simply being nosey? Will you be directly impacted? Does it even matter if you are? Do you feel led by the Holy Spirit to intervene? Every situation is different, friends. Pray for discernment.

PRAYER

Father God, thank You for creating me in Your image. Thank You for eyes to see, ears to hear, and a brain to think. I pray that You place in me a renewed sense of discernment, and a desire to please and glorify You in all of my words and actions. Give me the wisdom to keep my eyes forward, and to only let them stray into the lane of another when guided and prompted by Your Holy Spirit. Lord, let me honor You in all of my interactions, with love being the only motivation. Amen.

PRAYER
(write your own)

_____

_____

_____

_____

_____

_____

_____

_____

_____

Commute Encounters

From a Stranger

SCRIPTURE
*John 15:12-13, Philippians 2:3-4, Matthew 25:44-45,
Hebrews 13:2, John 13:34-35*

Today was a busy day in the Jacobsen household. My to-do list was piling up, and I was incredibly far behind in my chores and projects. My husband was getting ready to go out of state for a five-day military training and I was not prepared for him to leave.

I was feeling rushed to get everything done, and still spend as much time with my husband as I could before he left. The last thing I wanted to do in this moment was be away from him and my son, but naturally, that's exactly what I did.

My church was having their annual spring conference for the women's ministry, and I had registered to go. As much as I wanted to spend that time at home with my husband and son, my spiritual life needed feeding. My mother had made plans to go to the conference as well, so this was also a great opportunity to spend time with her.

We enjoyed a time of worship and teaching together, as well as some fellowship with other women in the church. We had an exceptional time together, but by the end of it, I was very tired and ready to be home.

As my mother and I left the church building and stepped out into the cool night air, I started thinking through the rest of my night.

It will probably be close to an hour before I get home. It's a 30-minute drive to my mom's house to drop her off, and then it will take me another 15 minutes or so to get home. We're leaving at 9pm, so I'll get home around 10pm or so. That'll leave time for a quick bite to eat and a hot shower before bedtime. Good plan Linz, good plan.

My mother and I settle into my SUV and start making our way towards the dark country roads that will lead us back home. Everything around us is still, and the world is in the process of settling down for the night. Her and I were both fairly exhausted, but we still managed to work in some conversation.

I filled her in on how my (this) book was going and bounced my chapter and title ideas off of her. I told her I currently had 10 chapters in the works, and she was beyond excited for me and eager to hear more about my concepts. I began to explain them to her as we slowed to a stop behind a car at a stop sign. We had been following this car for a little while now, but I didn't think anything special of it.

That is, until the driver put the car in park and opened up their car door. As soon as I saw them begin to step out, I put my car in reverse without hesitation and backed away. I kept my eyes glued on that open door, not daring to put my mother and myself at any risk.

The driver stepped out, and to my surprise, it was an elderly woman. I took quick mental note of her appearance. She was wearing a floral dress that reached down to her ankles. Her white hair was done up in a long braid, and her darkened eyes peered out from behind a pair of purple glasses. Now facing us, she waved her arms above her head, trying to draw our attention.

I rolled down my window and simply called out "Yes?" She then called back that she was lost and needed help. She kept her arms up in the air as she spoke, displaying her innocence, surely sensing my hesitancy.

You read about this sort of thing in a horror story, right? The classic "I need help" lure ...the seemingly innocent elderly woman needs help; oh, won't you please get out of your car and make yourself vulnerable?

I put my car in park and sat there in silence for a moment, just staring at this woman in my headlights. I let out of breath, then turned to my mother and told her to stay in the car. I swung my door open and tentatively approached the woman, scanning her car and my surroundings - mama didn't raise no fool.

I asked if she was trying to get to a store or business, as I quickly recalled the places that I knew of nearby. Her soft eyes met mine, and she said in a subtle, defeated voice, "I'm just trying to get back home."

As it turns out she had been visiting someone in Iowa and had gotten turned around in the country backroads and became lost. The road she sought was an interstate about 15-20 minutes away that would take her over a bridge to Illinois where she lived. She had apparently stopped once already to ask someone for directions. Whoever it was, gave her some fairly poor instructions, and she had become even more lost. Judging by the direction we had all just been traveling, she was heading in the exact opposite direction, getting even further and further from home.

I went back to my car and grabbed my cellphone. I figured this would be a quick fix sort of thing, where I could pull up my GPS and show her a map. So that's exactly what I did. I pulled up the maps and showed her where we currently were, and a few different paths she could take to get to the interstate. I showed her main roads, backroads, anything and everything I could think of that could help her.

She nodded as I explained things to her, but the fear in her eyes betrayed her. I realized then that my explanations were only confusing her more. I was overwhelming her with so much information, I was basically asking her to unravel a massive plate of word spaghetti.

Still, she seemingly appeared to understand what I was saying. Needing a second to gather my thoughts, I told her I would be right back and I walked back to my car. My mother was watching me with concerned eyes and I explained to her the woman's situation. My mom took a moment to process, then lowered her voice and said "why don't you just lead her?"

I could feel my face flush as my mother's idea sunk in. This woman was obviously in need of help, and I was more than capable of helping her. In that moment, did I truly believe that my verbal guidance would be enough to get her home? Did I trust in my own words enough to ensure this woman's safety? In that moment, no. I absolutely did not.

I held my mother's gaze for a second longer, then walked back over to the woman. I told her if she were willing to follow, then I would lead her to the interstate which would take her home.

The woman's jaw slipped ajar for just a brief second before a look of relief fell upon her face. "Bless your heart!" she responded, as her eyes gave off a soft glisten. I smiled and told her to let me get ahead of her in my car, and for her to just simply follow me. She nodded and returned to her car.

I took my time with the drive and made sure she was able to stay close to me, subtly reassuring her that I would not abandon her. After about 15 minutes, we made our way out of the country roads and back into the main of town. We found the exit for the interstate leading to Illinois, and we made our way onto it.

As I drove towards Illinois with the woman still in tow, I couldn't help but chuckle under my breath a little bit. Here, I had started my day out already having reservations about attending the conference, but I had decided to attend anyway. Then, I had left the church with full intention of heading North, and now here I am driving South!

Continuing along the interstate, a "Last Iowa Exit" sign came into view. I was fully prepared to cross the bridge into Illinois, but before I knew it, the woman pulled her car up next to me in the adjacent lane. I stole a glance over at her, to which she returned my gaze and smiled. She honked her horn a couple of times, waved, and then pulled ahead of me. Taking that as an indication that she had found her way, I waved and honked back; forever sealing my departing bond with this stranger.

I took the final Iowa exit and turned my car around. My mother and I road in silence for a while, each contemplating the things that had just unfolded. After a few modest moments, I couldn't help but blurt out "Well, I guess I have a chapter 11 now!". We shared a laugh, and I prayed out loud for the Lord to show me what the lesson was here. I knew it would sure be a good one that would linger with me a bit longer than the others.

Even now, almost a year later (and selecting it as my final chapter), I type it dwelling on the words of my mother that night: *"why don't you just lead her?"* It's such a simple statement and sentiment, but it's also an incredibly convicting one. Anybody can offer up words, but not everyone is willing to take action.

Scripture calls us to love one another. It also tells us to look into the interests of others, and to do nothing out of selfish ambition. When we hear of a friend or family member struggling, we typically will share some words of encouragement and a prayer with them, and then move on. If I dare to say it, I would bet that that is the default mentality setting engrained in many minds of those in the church (myself included).

Imagine what the church body would look like if we took Scripture more seriously and exchanged our words for action. If we let love be our charge, just picture what the body of Christ could do.

INVITE HIM IN

How often do we see an opportunity to display the love of Christ, and choose to pass over it? Whether it be for a stranger or a friend, even the smallest of things could have a significant impact. What would the world look like if we actively chose to make every conscious decision as if Jesus were standing there right next to us? That is quite the intimidating thought, but it sure is a humbling one.

Today, I challenge you to dig into Scripture and find at least five definitions and/or examples of what love looks like. Write the Scripture references below. Next, think of someone in your life who you can or need to love more actively. Write their name (or initials) below, and reach out to them as soon as you finish this chapter. Place a checkmark next to their name once you have done so.

1._____
2._____
3._____
4._____
5._____

Name:_____

PRAYER

Father God, thank You for showing us what love is. Thank You for displaying it for us through Jesus on the cross. Thank You for consistently showing us Your endless love through even the smallest of daily experiences. I pray that I can serve as an example of Your love to others around me through my words and actions. Lord, give me the wisdom, courage and clarity in these examples of love to reflect who You are. I pray that love will be my charge, and that I would have the boldness to display love more daringly. Amen.

PRAYER

(write your own)

_____
_____
_____
_____
_____
_____
_____
_____
_____
_____

Dear Reader,

You made it! You have read through all 14 commute encounters! Pat yourself on the back. Do a fun dance. Say "I did it" in a high-pitched voice. Order a milkshake! No matter what mini celebration you do, just know that you're awesome. Thank you for taking this journey with me. I truly appreciate you taking the time to read about my experiences with my commute time and with the Lord.

I would also like to take this opportunity to share with you who Jesus is, and how you too can receive the redeeming salvation that He offers.

We are all sinners, and are in desperate need of saving. Due to our evil, sinful nature, a gap was formed between us and God, our Creator. He is holy and pure, while we are broken and messy. Due to this imbalance, we have been separated from God, and our path was leading to death and eternal separation from Him.

But God, our loving Father, loved us *so* much, that He sent his son, Jesus, to earth to redeem us. Jesus lived a blameless, sinless life and chose to surrender his holiness to bear our sinful burden. He died a brutal, horrific death on the cross in our place. God's wrath and the penalty of death was laid on him, in an ultimate display of love. Satan and all of hell celebrated, thinking they had won, as Jesus breathed His last breath.

However, three days later, Jesus rose from the grave! He conquered death and ascended into heaven to be reunited with the Father. He paid the ransom for us, and became the bridge reconnecting the gap between us and God. The gift of salvation now being offered to us for free.

Like any gift, it only becomes yours once you actually accept and receive it. God offers His gift of forgiveness and redemption to us, but it only becomes ours once we accept the life of Jesus and embrace His work on the cross for us.

Reader, you can have the opportunity today to surrender your life to Jesus Christ and accept God's free gift of salvation. The healing power that comes from the Lord is unmatched. Take my word for it.

If this is something you want; if you want Jesus to come into your life and take the reins, then take some time right now to pray to God. Confess that Jesus is Lord. Confess your sins and sinful nature. Confess that you need saving through the sacrifice Jesus made for you.

The Lord is leaning in, dear reader. I pray that you lean in too and humble yourself before Him. Be honest. Be open. Let your life be transformed.

Here is a sample prayer to give you a little guidance.

Father God. I admit, I am a sinner. I know my sin has separated me from you. Lord, thank you for sending Jesus to earth to be the Savior of the world. With His death on the cross, He paid for the price of sin. Scripture says that whoever believes in Him will not perish, but have everlasting life. I want that Lord. I believe in Jesus, and the work that he accomplished. I ask for Christ to come into my life, and I surrender it fully to You. I know you can do a miraculous work, God, and I wait expectantly for it. I pray for guidance in my newfound faith, and I pray that You will give me the encouragement I need, in whatever form that may look like. Thank you, Father. Thank you for claiming me as Yours. Amen.

Psst ...have you prayed yet?

AWESOME!

I am <u>insanely</u> proud of you! Absolutely **INSANELY** proud of you!!! You just made the BEST decision of your life, and let me be the first to welcome to the family! My treasured brother or sister, welcome. You are so loved.

Now, good news needs to be shared. I would encourage you to share your life change with a family member or friend. Share it with someone at your church, or I ask that you even find me on social media and send me a message! I would love nothing more!

Thank you for taking this journey with me, reader. I am overwhelmed with joy that you chose to pick up my book and take a glimpse into the work the Lord has done in my life. I am so blessed to have been able to share it with you.

I will see you soon, friend. If not on this side of Heaven, then the other.

In Him,

Lindsay Jacobsen

Made in the USA
Columbia, SC
27 November 2021

49634314R00078